VANILLA NOW AND LATER

A Re-Introduction To The Grace Of Our Feminine Being

Tina P. Norton

VANILLA NOW AND LATER

Editorial Review and Book Layout – Spirit & Life Productions, a division of Norton Ministries, Inc., Marlton, NJ

Cover Design – JAK Studios, Seattle, WA

Scripture quotations are from the following versions:

> The Message Bible
> The Living Bible
> The New King James Version
> The New American Standard Bible
> The New International Version Bible

To my husband, thank you
for being a gentleman.

Foreword

In this 21st Century, Rev. Tina Norton is one of the most authentic, courageous, and anointed women of God who runs after God and His vision. Her life is exemplary of the prepared and educated woman who is undaunted by the many challenges she faces in ministry with her husband, Sr. Pastor Curtis Norton of Merrick Park Baptist Church in Jamaica, NY. Executive Pastor Tina presents her audience with tremendous opportunities for other woman to reflect and rediscover their own authentic place in God. Tina is very insightful in the many intriguing metaphors she uses in this manuscript that allows us to examine our own relationship with God throughout each season of our lives.

Tina's message is unique and powerful as she manifests essential principles for living an abundant life in Christ. Some of these principles include living life free of fear, scars, and the toxic behaviors that rob us of our destiny and destination. By the time this book is published, you will have witnessed a revelation and a prophetic word as it pertains to empowering women to experience emotional and theological wholeness.

It is my hope, reality and vision that this ministry will begin to address Liberation and Justice for women across the country.

Dr. Phyllis E. Carter
M.S., LCMFT., M.Div., D.Min.

Table of Contents

Introduction

What glorious grace our God has bestowed upon us as He, in creation made us sexual beings. In His image and likeness we were created; this includes our sexuality. It was not an afterthought in the mind of God nor was it the result of our sin nature. In the Book of Beginnings, sex is a part of the original, perfect creation of mankind. Our feminine grace is in God's image. Created after the animals, male and female are the only ones God referred to as being in His image. We therefore are a different class of being...not mere animals. We don't share their primitive instincts nor do we lack the ability to responsibly control our urges. Unlike them, we were created for relationship with God and with each other. We were created to be one - spirit, soul, and body. This mystery is the divine fusion of our triune being in the awesome grace of covenant, sexual expression; man and woman – naked and not ashamed.

What a great gift we possess in the godly revelation of our sexual being. Attached to our being is Divine purpose; all of the Fathers' work in and on us is good. We must exalt our status to the mind of Christ concerning us and begin to change our attitude to the picture of who He says we are. There is no clear image in the earth today of the godly woman in her "full bodied" savor as she is the feminine expression of the salt of the earth. The creation of woman by God is too intelligent to be just another pretty face or a sensuous Mona Lisa silhouette. There is too much stock in us for such a superficial rendering. Our essence, who we are, is so much more than that. We are often plastered on display for the purpose of showing forth our ability to model beauty. Is that the limit of our ability? I say not! This is not enough for the sister who has decided to be all that God has destined for her to become. She cannot simply model beauty, she must possess it. According to Dr. Myles Monroe, the definition of purpose is "the original intent for the creation of a thing that was in the mind of the creator of a thing". When God made us He made us good.

Too often we get stuck on yesterday at the

expense of our glorious future. I begin here to reaffirm why Always A Lady became a theme for my life and how important it is to secure this present fullness of revelation for me and so many others; especially this generation, as we seek to preserve the sacred purpose of our God-given purity and address the enemy's onslaught of it. Our personal deliverance is truly as personal as our ownership of it. We can't bury our heads in the sand and hope that the difficult seasons in our lives never existed. We must determine to learn from and categorize them for our personal development as well as there potential impact for others. This is the confrontation with our history, the assault, the secret(s) and our rescue by the mighty hand of God. The journey is indeed worth the effort necessary to map out the path to victory.

It was in 1962 that the Phoenix Candy Company came out with the Now and Later bar and it sent kids wild. Each Now and Later bar consisted of several individually wrapped taffy squares, and the bars were available in close to fourteen flavors. The name was selected to suggest to customers that they eat some of the taffy squares in the bar right away and save the rest for another occasion.

The Phoenix Company goes back to 1919, when a little candy company in Brooklyn, New York, was turning out penny saltwater taffy. In 1953, the company became the Phoenix Candy Company, which struck gold with its popular product. The candy brand has been owned and made by several companies between that time and today, including Beatrice Foods, Hershey and currently Farley & Sather's Candy of Minneapolis.

There are fifteen flavors available today and the eight most popular old time favorites which are all fruit flavors. Often asked about are the chocolate and vanilla flavors... unfortunately they are no longer made.

Little did I know that Vanilla Now & Later would be my call to address the awesome grace of femininity that God destined for us as we walk toward the fulfillment of divine destiny. It is presently our call to abandon anything that has held us back as we are commissioned to come into the light of our marvelous purpose. There is no weapon created (it can never be manufactured) that has the capacity to prosper against us. Our purity is the will of God!

This is our call to secure the mindset that will stabilize our restored place as our God has set the captive free. This long-awaited deliverance is our new platform for breakthrough for all generations....life now is sweet and my joy is complete for I'm saved, saved, saved... fully restored and made whole by the precious blood of the Lamb.

Section 1 – The Journey Up The Stairs

Chapters One – Four:

It is the fall of '67, at six years of age I am a student at Public School 100 on 139th Street between Lenox and Fifth Avenues in Harlem, USA. My life is as normal as any other young girl, bright eyed and bushy tailed, excited about a fresh start for the school year. I was a better than average student from the very start – all of my siblings were. I loved school and the prospect of learning. I was truly excited about it all. It's funny; I'm still pretty much the same way. As a result of this, I was often chosen to take the attendance record to the school principal. The custom was that two students were selected daily as this was one of the highlights of the day, in addition to recess (which by the way replaced the kindergarten nap time - that for me was hard to overcome).

On this particular November morning, two precious little girls were sent to the principal's office to hand in the attendance sheet.

Section 1 – The Journey Up The Stairs

As on any other occasion, we proudly clicked our Buster Brown™ oxfords down the marbled corridor on to the stairs to complete our special assignment. I can still vividly see the caged stairwell that didn't seem as intriguing that day as it does today in my mind's eye. Life takes you through stages that cause you to revisit things in a very unusual way. Like most public or government buildings, upon reflection, the stairwell can be a very scary place. The cage or fence that framed the banister along the up and down of the stairs, now…as then became the prison that attempted to lock me in to a fight for my future. I didn't realize it then but I had begun a journey that would take me over many years of living according to a certain pattern of thinking that was rooted in the awful events of that fall day. On the way back from the attendance office we were confronted by two young men who barricaded us in the stairwell. They kept saying things like, 'we were pretty', they wanted to touch us, they wanted to play…the older man (who was sitting at the top of the stairs) in particular was doing most of the talking, while the younger one was blocking the steps. With crystal clear recollection, this scene plays out in my head. The feeling was very strange as I tried to decipher what was going on in my six year old mind. I was perplexed with the rush of emotion and fear that engulfed me. I was seemingly frozen in time as the other young girl who was with me was released because she started crying and squalling loudly. I was left to ward off these advances as he offered me candy if I let him touch me; the exchange – "you're so pretty, come on…let me touch you, I'll give you this candy" – it was Vanilla Now & Later.

What do you do in moments like that? How do you handle the uneasiness that you feel while trying to determine your next move? In shock, what fuels your emotion while you attempt to read the many mixed signals you're confronted with? It was leap years ahead that I would be reacquainted with this suppressed event and in a déjà vu moment, confronted with memories that spanned thirty plus years and began to explain why I was and did much of what I chose to do over my life. The decision to take the high road in life was produced out of this experience. The choice between the Happy Meal and the Market Price Meal of life was solidified there; it all began to make sense. This just could not be how a lady was to be approached. Something wasn't right about it.

1. The Point of Decision

Fear

There is no fear in love. But perfect love drives out fear, because fear has to do with punishment. **"The one who fears is not made perfect in love."** 1 John 4:18 NIV

Children are generally fearless. Their innocent view of their surroundings and the people who occupy them is so tender. Bright-eyed and bushy-tailed they enter life on their own terms as they set out on a quest for information and new things to conquer. They are an interesting subject, carefree and fanciful. All of us have had the experience of talking to a seemingly brilliant child and wondered if they had been here before. We tend to encourage (or should) the dialogue and inquisitiveness of these children. We also guard them as we've come to understand, they have to be directed into truths as we harness their strengths. It's a terrible thing when their precious innocence is disrupted by the thievery of life's mishaps. Cut right into their foundation, the enemy's plan can and often prevails as they are simply pursuing proper footing.

There is nothing new under the sun. The devil's plans are tried and tested. He began them from the foundation of the world, when he challenged God himself. He's never learned his lesson. He went on to tempt Adam and Eve in the garden, and throughout history he has been working diligently – seeking whoever he may devour. He even tried to attack our Savoir and was reminded of the power of the Word of God. Every person with destiny attached to their lives is susceptible to his devices. The scripture declares he has come to kill, steal, and destroy. He starts very early in his attempt to abort the Father's plan for our lives. If he is not successful in one area, he'll try another and another – it goes on and on until he is ultimately found out. This is why we must protect ourselves from his insidious assault, however if we were unaware of these truths over seasons in our lives, we tend to lack preparedness as to how to thwart them. Especially as youngsters, it is here where we are most vulnerable. If the hedge around us is penetrated we spiral into a life of fear and instability. Generally speaking, we are subject to a viewpoint that stops at our point of despair. If we are not assisted in this area, we carry unnecessary burdens that clouded seasons in our lives produced. The devil doesn't play fair. This is what I know. I am reminded of when I made a knee-jerk decision that I didn't like the atmosphere that my own encounter with darkness presented. It began a journey in which I settled, early on – how I would handle my own life. I needed to avoid the uneasiness that that moment presented and as a young girl of six years, I made up my mind that I would never accept the advances of a man that weren't appropriate. In that moment, I was branded with something I could not explain until many years later. That moment in time shook my future and declared my Father's Will when I could barely comprehend it.

Fear is an awful thing; its emotion runs the gamut of many feelings that manifest in very horrible ways. It is an emotional response to threats and danger. It is a basic survival mechanism occurring in response to a specific stimulus, such as pain or the threat of pain. Most psychologists suggest that fear is one of a small set of innate emotions. They include joy, sadness, and anger. In fear, one may go through various emotional stages. A good example of this is the cornered rat, which tries to run away until it is finally cornered by its predator at which point it will become belligerent and fight back with heavy aggression until it either escapes, or is captured. The same goes for most animals. Humans however, can become very intimidated by fear, causing them to go along with another's wishes without regard to their own input. Our reaction to fear is fueled by rising adrenaline levels, rather than a consciously thought-out decision.

The physiological effects of fear are very different in that they are measured in our nervous response to either fight or take flight. The rush of physical changes manifest in muscles changes, perspiration and protective measures that ward off the attack.

We are sometimes arrested under the grip

of fear when we are uncertain about a problem or circumstance that presents itself as we seek to move forward with a decision. It is funny because life is in itself a series of decisions we must make that help us evolve and mature. We cannot run away from making choices, even where fear resides. Have you ever had the instance when someone wasn't sure about what they wanted, let's say for dinner as you where out at a restaurant and they asked you, "What should I get?" You are stuck with their indecision as your next question is usually something like, "what do you have a taste for?" we are always making decisions. The truth is they decided to ask you what they should eat. Usually in decision making, there are some basic principles we each have to incorporate like: the facts that are before us, how your choice affects or impacts your decision, and what that which you are questioning entails. This is all further complicated by the type of decision you are making and is sometimes stifled when one is afraid. It's easy to want to clock out during this process because it requires serious thought as we peruse the options.

If fear rules this process the ultimate decision is generally not successful. This is why it is difficult for many to walk out their faith appropriately when life has dealt only mishaps and despair. If I've bumped into enough walls in life I've got to fight as I learn to leap over those walls. I am convinced there are levels of fear that we conquer. When I think of the near assault on my life in that school stairwell, I remember the raw emotion of my six years of age and now understand that I didn't have the tools then to process what I could not pinpoint. Driven by fear, I was in no position to determine my fate. Some portion of the experience is then suppressed as it is shelved until we are equipped to handle it. There is no timeframe on this. For some people it is short but for others it can take a lifetime. Still for others, additional help is necessary to overcome the trauma that brick walls bring. Fear comes to attack the process of decision making and annihilate our trust as we are to believe God for our life and future. The enemy of our soul starts early in our lives to sabotage the lifelong decision making process. This is how he works his attempt to abort our destiny. If he can disrupt the foundation of our beginning, he keeps his finger in the crack that remains.

We can be assured for God has not given us a spirit of fear. What the devil meant for our destruction our Father promised to turn it around for our good. He has given us a spirit of love, a spirit of power, and a sound mind. And perfect love cast out all fear.

Déjà vu

I strongly believe that all of our life has significance. There is not one moment, stage, or season that does not relate in some manner to another. Life is really a cycle of events and occurrences that mold and shape us in many ways. Our character is shaped by these instances. The way we view the world is part of the outflow of these matters. Our successes and our failures can directly be tied to how we've processed various seasons of our existence and applied the lessons learned in those times based on the good and the bad we've gleaned. Everything is relative. How we mentally store this information is very complex. I am not at all qualified to speak to those complexities; however I do know that our human make-up has shown me some consistent patterns in our lives. We tend to store situations in our lives by levels of intensity. Generally, a more traumatic occurrence can be buried in our subconscious and never completely dealt with. Its outflow tends to manifest without ever addressing the root of the challenge one may have faced. Smaller or less significant problems we meet are usually processed in a swifter mode of operation, probably because it doesn't require a lot of effort. The intensity of the challenge determines for most of us how long we'll spend defending our right to overcome it. Let's be honest, none of us like the idea of confrontation; let alone when it's with our selves. I am convinced that God did not awake on any given day unaware of what each of us would encounter for that day. First off, He neither slumbers nor sleeps. Secondly, He has orchestrated every season of our lives, even to the minutest detail. He has always been for us, never against us. From the be-ginning, His plan promises us a great future.

Have you ever had a time in your life that you strangely felt that you were set back in a time capsule where you had been in one sea-son or another? You shake yourself trying to recall the eerie feeling of... I know what's go-ing to happen or this feels very familiar. You begin to draw conclusions that somehow prove that you're not just in the moment – it's at-tached to something else, usually bigger than that time. It's the kind of thing that happens when all of the pieces seem to come together; a this is for that moment. It's almost like the missing piece of the puzzle, when portions of your life somehow, suddenly make more sense. I call it the "aha" moment, some re-fer to it as déjà vu. The difference between the two is small but telling. To me, the "aha" moment is a soft wind that blows on a mo-ment in your life that answers the why of that season. It is a peace that comes which settles us while we reconcile the enlightenment. It's like the recording of an event that enlightens you from a place you've longed and searched for and suddenly the light comes on. Déjà vu is an uncanny feeling or illusion of having already seen or experienced something that is being experienced. This phenomenon is just that, it generally settles nothing. We have all experienced a feeling that comes over us occasionally, of what we are saying and doing having been said and done before, in a remote time – of our having been surrounded, dim ages ago, by the same faces, objects, and circumstances – of our knowing perfectly what will be said next, as if we suddenly remember it (Charles Dickens)! It is that already lived – already felt feeling that jolts us; yet draws no relevant conclusions.

Sometimes, when we've experienced traumatic times in our lives we suppress the feelings associated with them. This can manifest when we don't have the capacity to handle all that we've encountered, especially if we were younger. Every crisis is further layered upon another, until we're seemingly buried underneath. So much can hinder our forward progress if we aren't equipped with the proper mechanisms to decipher the course of our lives. Many have had the fierce wind of adversity blow on their pleasant day and disrupt the frame of their life. We journey onward, sometimes directionless, until we encounter revelations that assist us on our path. Life must make sense to us if we are to grow and prosper. We all long for that peace be still moment we deserve.

The Scar(s)

We all have scars. They are the markers in our lives that recall the bumps that got us over the rough times. In the Greek the word for scar is eschara, meaning place of fire or fireplace. It is the intense burning in our soul that is a perpetual reminder of the pain associated with an event in our lives; like the flickering ambers that sting us as the fire pops and kindles. There is an ebb and flow to the pain of a healing scar much like the changing colors of the fire's flame. When the actual abrasion begins its natural healing, it often hurts as much as when you originally had the incident. A scar results as this is a natural part of the healing process.

Skin scars occur when the deep, thick layer of skin (the dermis) is damaged. The worse the damage is, the worse the scar will be. What's first natural is also spiritual. Many of us have experienced surface attacks that we found easily remedied. Much of life we just brushed off like it was no big deal, but the other stuff that cuts deeper to our core is what we struggle with. We fight tooth and nail to break free from the agony of certain seasons in our lives only to be confronted with their nagging pull at our soul...the ever burning fire.

Most skin scars are flat, pale and leave a trace of the original injury that caused them. However, from a spiritual standpoint, we learn to look away from these reminders as we fail to confront the original injury. This is not healthy. The redness that often follows an injury to the skin is not a scar, and is generally not permanent. The time it takes for it to go away may, however, range from a few days to, in some serious and rare cases, a few years. It's difficult to reconcile our individual encounter with these seasons in our lives.

How quickly we address them is generally not a factor as is how effectively we deal with the root of how we walk them out. Spiritually, this process can't be avoided. Various treatments can speed up the natural process in serious cases, however time is often the best spiritual healer as the Blood of Jesus is our promise for breakthrough.

Scars form differently based on the location of the injury on the body and the age of the person who was injured, but a scar is a scar. Nobody's a cry baby when it comes to the challenges that life throws at us – if it hurts cry. We can't minimize another's despair. We must empathize with one another and push (sometimes gently) us toward healing. There is a Balm in Gilead!

To mend the damage, the body has to lay down new collagen fibers (a naturally occurring protein that is produced by the body). In the mending process the body cannot rebuild the tissue exactly as it was, so the new scar tissue will have a different texture and quality than the surrounding normal tissue. However, we can choose to look at it in a more positive way. The scars in my life should not be reflected upon and cause the original pain of that season of my being. An injury does not become a scar until the wound has completely healed and scar tissue can be as good as the normal tissue it replaces. Let the healing begin…don't make your scar a trophy.

There comes a point when the scars of life need our permission to permanently go away. On any given day I can look at the cut on my right elbow and tell you exactly what happened. However, the nine stitches that mark the place of the original pain and the mental image of the incident don't hurt anymore. Now I need to move on as this scar becomes my teacher in my new season. Its lessons instruct me to avoid the bad decision I made in the first place. In addition to this, my report card now monitors my progress in the class called, 'How to Avoid the Dumb Stuff'. This scar now makes me laugh and my joy is the trophy I uphold!

Vulnerability

Emotional hurt and pain is more than

psychological. It is very spiritual in nature. Dependant upon one's access to strong and healthy guidance, this can make or break an individual's progress in their journey to wholeness. Feelings of being taken advantage of or abused generate weakness. One is usually susceptible to the emotional pain associated with their suffering. We become fragile and sometimes unresponsive as we go through life. Some have called it 'shutting down' or 'clocking out of life'; hiding from what we cannot handle. You feel entrapped or imprisoned in a situation where your feelings or rights are ignored. Opening yourself up to others is difficult as you never want to experience the feeling of being taken advantage of. No one wants their despair turned back on them if they open up their innermost feelings and fears to someone else; so we stop trusting people. It's sad when people use such feelings and fears against you. I've found that hurting people hurt others. This is often because they've never confronted their personal despair. Vulnerability is a cage that immobilizes our emotions, feelings, and actions.

1. The Point of Decision

We've got to learn to free ourselves from the oppressions we find hard to release. There is no growth or possibility of enlarging yourself to explore other emotional and spiritual dimensions when you allow an instance in your life to forever hold you captive. We must fight for our future. I refuse to allow my personal growth and development to be hindered by the devil's plot to kill me. Remember, the thief comes to kill, steal, and destroy but Jesus said, **"I have come that you may have life and that more abundantly"**. He's our Strong Deliverer! As we begin to breakout of our caged past, we give way to a new pathway to victory. Get new friends, change your behavior, adjust your attitude and give yourself a fighting chance. Unrelenting pursuit of oneself is a healthy way to say no to life's setbacks. You must declare, "I will survive". It's all how you choose to view it. Welcome honest feedback from new associations, not just those who agree with you or have similar experiences. Even the negative is positive if it's folded into your growth and enlargement. Abandon the need to be absolutely sure of the outcome of your newfound liberty. Free yourself to accept what you can not change and decide to step up to the new elevation freedom brings. Declare to yourself, I am coming out!

2. Mixed Signals

Her-story

Everyone has history, whether upon broken planks that carried you over or the cannonball blast that catapults you into your glorious future; we all have a story to tell. It is likely that each our lives are cut off from the Master's fabric with definite markings that we meet along life's trail. The Father set a course for us from the foundation of the world. His plans entail the whole of our existence as He mapped out our expected end and then back tracked to set our beginning. Nothing in our life is a surprise to Him; the good, the bad, or the indifferent. Somewhere etched in our heavenly existence is the complete picture of all we are to become; before we were bodily, we were spirit. The Lord's quest in us is to get us reconnected to Him as He unveils His divine purpose along the way. He told us in the Bible, I know the plans I have for you, plans to make you prosper and give you hope as well as a marvelous expected end.

2. Mixed Signals

Every negative in life is set to divert us from the Lord's best for us. Life can be tough. The journey is filled with winding roads and narrow paths. There are no concrete course directions, let alone the changing landscape of our individual existence. Sometimes it seems as if it's every man for him self. It's a wonder many make it. There is the potential for serious misreads along the road of life, some of which we never recover from. I know I'm talking right. Each of us has had to buckle down our life focus and pay attention to the things we encounter on a daily basis. We've learned over time that this is the best way to avoid pitfalls. I call this living life on purpose; you've heard the saying, "don't be an accident going somewhere to happen." History has shown us that a failure to prioritize our course leads to reckless wanderings to nowhere. Aren't we tired of that?

Most people avoid the clear signals that pop up in front of the junctures life's course presents. Gone are the days we choose to operate on basic self-survival, insecurities, and lack of self confidence. We need direction for our lives and the only one who can truly help us is our Creator – He's got the blueprint. Our indecision concerning Him stalls our forward progression as we wait on someone or something else to validate our next move. We give our lives over to so many other things as we get lost in the sauce of day to day living. Fear of the unknown or uncharted waters paralyzes us, as we float along effortlessly hoping to bump into something, anything, meaningful. Lack of forgiveness and the inability to forget past hurts, injustices, and pain stifle us, rendering us ineffective. Sadly, this is just what the enemy wants, to hold us hostage to our original pains or fears.

Observations – Lessons from Others

I've spoken with so many people, especially women who've just thrown in the towel of life. Young and older, they want nothing to do with what will assist them with getting back on course. The overwhelming need for personal privacy and repressed confidences smother them like a baby's precious security blanket.

2. Mixed Signals

A life of denial ensues such that they convince themselves that all is well as they persevere toward nothingness. They refuse to face life head-on as it is what it is. Uncomfortable with change they settle - defiantly wearing the shell they've covered themselves with to protect their identity (or the one they don't know). Hardened by their life journey, they decide it's better to merely show up than to truly participate in life. They are convinced that life is a complete wash. With no energy left to wring out anything of substance, they choose to spin out of existence and never truly show-up.

I'm reminded of how that stairwell experience with almost being raped is what produced an emotional shutdown in my life. I was a very shy child in my own way attempting to draw back from any direct attention from others. It made me feel very uncomfortable. Shyness produces a hesitancy to meet new people, being a "wall flower" in social gatherings due to fear of rejection or fear of disapproval. I hoped no one noticed that I was around, how miserable. Those mixed signals that had left an apprehension in me could have continued the blinding effect it had on my life. I would have never opened up to others, nor released all the Father had in me for others.

Double-faced vs. Two-faced

Our unwillingness to unmask the two faces we portray bottles up our true self and has buried who we really are, what we are able to do, and who we are able to be. Looking good is far from the multi layers each of these faces produce. We begin to manifest two very similar presentations of ourselves. One is what I call double-faced and the other is two-faced. They are nearly the same but with stronger negative and hurtful details on the latter. Double faced is like having two faces or aspects to one's being. It is marked by deliberate deceptiveness especially by pretending one set of feelings and acting under the influence of another. This is usually a shield we put up. One tends to function on both sides, they are duplicitous. Two faced is slightly different in that it has two faces or surfaces and double deals with deceit. Skillful and cunning, once the veil is lifted people can't believe this was really you. There is a difference between deceptions for the mere purpose of disguising oneself to mask pain you don't know how to handle then deceit which deliberately adds on the greater element of trickery. Both of them are dishonest but being two-faced is more self destructive. It is tricky as one has mastered the false face to perfection that their brain operates at warp speed as they shift from face to face. They are smooth and calculating as they've so fooled themselves that they are convinced that everybody else is also fooled. We don't like to talk about this stuff because it's too much like truth. We run the risk of our own personal exposure of perpetrating actions that confuse and deceive others. This beast of burden carries a heavy load as one manipulates through life and rarely comes into one's own; thereby needing to downplay another's success. I've observed that depending on your level of discernment, you can read this effortlessly as you clearly see the brain sifting gears to switch to the "right face" for the moment;

how sad. On the offensive we operate sending the same mixed signals that captured us as we blame everyone but ourselves to avoid our personal spotlight.

We perfect the game so well that we convince ourselves that it's the truth until we are alone in our mess seeking something or someone to drown out our reality. These games involve knowing the rules of certain body language associated with different forms of social interaction and result in performance of routines and scripts that fit the "game". Game knows game but gamers hardly ever tell on themselves or the others in the game, they just perpetuate their game on those who fail to confront them. That's just too much work. You see, this pattern is played out regularly in the sisterhood whereby we are not in place to be our sister's keeper.

I have found that some people shut down their emotions by pleasing others. Some become silent observers of life frozen in time only to live a life that avoids warmth as they fear it will thaw them out. The lack of an emotional language or the ability to tune into their own feelings buried deep inside fosters their stagnation. I live by this motto, to thy own self be true; you don't have to convince anyone that you're as special as you are and it is okay if you need someone to help you.

3. Secrets & Shame

How Do We Bury the Nagging Inner Struggle?

It's time to put out the fire. It takes tremendous energy to hold onto secrets that keep us locked in shame. The time is now to let go of it all. I realize shame can permeate the core of one's being. It's not easy to let go of the past, but it is vitally necessary. Not only are some things hard to talk about, they are also difficult to revisit. Most of us would like to have a huge eraser that can wipe away various seasons in our lives but that doesn't exist. Upon reflection, we ask ourselves, why me? Did I bring this on myself? There is no answer to these questions that settle the heart and thereby leave a void that's often unfilled. It takes a genuine desire to be liberated from the pull deep within. It can take a long time to get to that stage, everyone is different. If you are apt to hold in your emotions, it's harder to release the secrets and shame. We bury the nagging struggle within while it continues to cry out to be released. Once the cry out weighs the pain, it becomes easier to deal with. The challenge is that we slowly get around to identifying what we want to do with letting go. Our life cannot remain at a stand still.

I remember ministering to a woman at a retreat who was seventy-eight years old and had been raped by a male relative. She never spoke of it. Like many others there was a silencer placed on her soul, in her case because it just wasn't spoken about in her generation. She is not a lot different from others I've spoken with, who because of being told not to tell or being threatened, never let it go. Sometimes we spend too much time trying to rationalize the why, that we close off to potential assistance for our breakthrough. No matter what your age expose the secret, healing can only come once you shed light on your despair. That scar needs the sunlight. Anytime the enemy 'has something' on you that no one else knows about, he milks that advantage over you until you are left was no strength. The minute you open up to a safe ear and a strong heart that can begin to walk you through to victory, the struggle dissipates. You also have to be prepared to release your offender which is not always as simple as it sounds. This is why you need to be careful that you share your heart with someone positioned to truly help you. There are deep soul wounds that have to be dealt with and the healing process begins with you deciding to let that deep place receive exposure to the light of a qualified healer.

The Bible teaches us in the story of Tamar how grievous an offense sexual assault is. There is nothing new under the sun. The king's daughters in their virginity were distinguished by "garments of divers colors". Tamar dressed in this finery as the beautiful, devoted daughter of David. She excelled in baking delicious cakes laced with spices like "cordials" which happened to be one of her brother's favorite. One day she was summoned to tend to her ill brother and to make him some cake. She was raped by Amnon, her half-brother who by encouragement from his friend Jonadab, helped plan this abominable plot. Amnon was David's oldest son and even though the law of Israel forbade incest

[Lev. 18:9, 11] the low estate of women during this era would not even withhold the choice he made toward his half-sister. Despite the fact that she wore the dress of a princess, "a long-sleeved garment," Amnon's servant treated her as a common woman and threw her out of his house. Tamar put ashes on her head, tore her royal dress, distraught – she ran for refuge to her brother Absalom's house. She remained there and lived in a state of widowhood. It was a couple of years later that this violation was avenged as Absalom's fury drives him to murder Amnon. The scriptures are full of these tragedies and so many other life challenges. Thank God for Jesus, He is our Mighty Avenger. His word shows us that our God is the only one who can bring forth our justice.

Many have suffered severe blows with stolen innocence and have been defrauded. Abuse in various forms has handicapped so many others. However, the grace of God is available for you! **"He heals the broken in heart and binds up their wounds"** Psalm 147:3; the Lord provides complete restoration! Wrapped up in salvation, our Lord has folded in beauty for ashes as he's come to set the captive free. **"The Spirit of the Lord God is upon me, because the Lord has anointed me to bring good news to the suffering and afflicted. He has sent me to comfort the brokenhearted, to announce liberty to captives, and to open the eyes of the blind. He has sent me to tell those who mourn that the time of God's favor to them has come, and the day of his wrath to their enemies. To all who mourn in Israel he will give: beauty for ashes; joy instead of mourning; praise instead of heaviness. For God has planted them like strong and graceful oaks for his own glory."** Isaiah 61:1-3. My sister, you are stronger than you think. The Lord wants to partner with you for your glorious future.

Shame

Don't let anyone or anything break your spirit. It is the vital link between your soul's efforts toward a whole heart. This is why the course of life must be dealt with because life can indeed either make or break you. In the early years of life anything can hinder the success of this growth. We are the sum total of all that has happened to each of us. Major attacks can knock us completely off life's building blocks. They shatter the project we were to become. Reclaiming the building's structure is not always easy as we try to hold on to what is covering us while still working to gather together the scattered pieces. Many get caught in the cycle of trying to overcome the painful emotion of shame. When life brings the type of circumstance that produces disgrace we tend to try to hide it. Those who suffer from shame are often left with feelings of inferiority and inadequacy that hinder their development. It appears that ones life has been censored like a classified file. There's this grave caution when opening the folder as its content is highly sensitive. Top Secret is the stamp on this shame.

How do you bury forever what needs a respectful ceremony? Whatever the infraction is, it has to be acknowledged at the level it affected the victim. It can't be swept away. In order to bury shame, I must look my offense straight in its face. I must call it what it is; the vile attempt of the enemy of my soul to abort my future destiny. I must then turn the attention within and release my soul to look and lash out at the infraction so as to have my last say. It is then and only then that the healing can begin. I also need the power of God and the precious Holy Spirit to guide me through the days ahead as I regain my footing upon the hope they give me. I learn to declare that my life is a sum of all my experiences and the lessons they each bring. There value is the cornerstone of my success as I learn to appreciate that I am who I am by the grace of God. I am responsible to guard my heart's health as my Sovereign God has granted me this authority, **"Make a tree good and its fruit will be good, or make a tree bad and its fruit will be bad, for a tree is recognized by its fruit. You brood of vipers, how can you who are evil say anything good? For out of the overflow of the heart the mouth speaks."** Matthew 12:33-34 NIV.

The Inner Child

The Inner Child is a concept used in popular psychology to denote the childlike aspect of a person's psyche, especially when it is viewed as an independent entity. I view it as that little place we curl up in within the secret place of the soul. It is usually the "safe place" of our existence; our security blanket. This orphan soul clings on to the familiar to avoid anything that will rock the boat. It is where everything is neatly placed and no one is allowed to disrupt it. Frequently, the term is used to address suppressed childhood experiences and the remaining effects of them. It is here that what we can't explain away or don't like to deal with is unconsciously agreed that we don't have to talk about it. It is our personal burial ground – the dark cemetery of the soul. The individual is even cautious about how they walk through it. It is here that the abandoned soul of our inner child stores all of the emotional memory and experiences in the brain from their earliest recollection. It is a place of torment. It is the living "dash" of our existence; the present place of our beginning and our end. It is so often here that we need to be healed from the addiction, abuse, and trauma of life. The child within must be delivered from the cemetery of their soul.

When one's heart has been broken it is sometimes difficult to mend. It requires intentional effort on the part of the one who seeks to be made whole. Just as it is in the natural, our heart is the major organ that sustains life. In the spiritual realm, our hearts health is just as important. We must guard our heart according to Proverbs 4:20-23, **"My son, pay attention to what I say; listen closely to my words. Do not let them out of your sight, keep them within your heart; for they are life to those who find them and health to a man's whole body. Above all else, guard your heart, for it is the wellspring of life."** When life deals you a bad hand you must play that hand to the best of your ability. It must be observed very carefully as it's played out until another hand or season is presented. How I view the game of life is determined by how well I keep my heart's health. That is to say, I must be attentive to what goes into my heart because its outflow is what the scriptures call the issues of life. When my heart is full of the right things my life will be successful. If I fail to guard my heart and I allow the bad things I've experienced to be harbored there, I will only produce negativity as its outflow.

The abandonment that the soul feels when life throws its rocks and hurdles should never tank us. We must encourage ourselves as we are renewed in the spirit of our mind. This will bring about the necessary healing required for growth and fulfillment. A healthy heart makes a healthy life. We are not boxed into the seasons of our lives. We are the victors not victims of our circumstance(s). I'm reminded of a quote by American Abolitionist and former Slave, Frederick Douglass who said, "The soul that is within me no man can degrade." This powerfully declares the position we must take as we are confronted with the eerie stairwell of life.

4. The Struggle

Hurting People Hurt

Life is a series of doors of opportunity that present themselves for personal growth and development. Our Creator formed each of us in our mother's womb long before she or our father knew we existed. The Lord fashioned us after he mapped out all of our days and backtracked to the beginning of our being. He then released us to earth when we were born. Our original birth date is in the mind of God who created everything and called it good. These life doors are along the course of the blueprint our Father has laid out for our life, and he requires us to check in with Him for a successful journey. Unfortunately, most of us are unaware or unwilling to submit to the direction of the Lord so we forfeit the peace a life lead by Him brings. As a result of this we struggle through life on our own course to nowhere in a desperate attempt to make something meaningful of it. Before long we get beat up and battered as pride prohibits us from seeking help from anyone, let alone the God who loves and created us. We end up hurt and abused by the course of life and perpetuate a cycle wherein hurting people hurt; and the cycle continues...

These are observations and lessons learned from others. It's what I call caged pain. I will not speak their names but I will speak their pain:

• **Hatred**...this is the spoon of emotion that only erodes the soul of the one who hates. It is a real emotion seemingly justified as the response to the most hideous attacks. I can't stand you and I don't know why.

• She stepped out of her body never to return. It was there she left who she had become to that point, unwilling to deal with how this would impact who she was. Now she says, I'll just be someone else; **denial** - is that me?

• Busy seeking to satisfy everyone in every instance, everywhere... I am an **enabler**. Since I've been bombarded and invaded, I let others have their way with me. I forfeit the fight in me as it seems easier to give in — I give up!

- The **extreme** I am — you see, I'm hurt so I hurt everyone I can. No one gets one up on me – it's either kill or be killed. I'm shut all the way down – it's dark in here...

- The home front, which is supposed to be a safe place, for me it's my ball of confusion. At my friend's house things are different — sanity, whatever that means. It is here, I begin to lose it as a lack of solid structure cripples my personal development — I'm **unprepared**, so life for me is haphazard.

- **Utopia** is what I want life to be. Mine has been unfair. I'm not happy because of it all. I have everything, yet I possess nothing. I am on a search for meaning with substance — something needs to stick. Until then, I'm stuck so I feed my addiction as it is the one thing I can depend on to escape to there...

- There's no rest for the weary soul, is there? I'm a **zombie** – can't get it out of my mind so I wrestle in my night bed awakened by summer's early arrival. I wasn't ready, and now I'm so tired. This is stolen youth which was forced to grow before she was grown. The silent treatment, shhh — hush up child, we don't talk about stuff like that...go to your room. It will be all right in the morning. My daylight never comes.

• These feet were made for walking, and I'm getting out of here. I am **unstable**; I escape my reality as I don't like sinking roots. That's too much like stability, and I'm not comfortable with it. I change everything around me — often. You'll never be able to mark my tracks — I glide...

• I'm a **controller**...I'm gonna stay on top. I'm so ate up with the need to be everybody's boss that I'll murder whoever gets in my way; I'm cool and calculating, it's my way or no way. Somewhere in life I picked up this spirit and it has worked for me this long I'm convinced I'm right. I don't know but I feed on the energy that control fuels. It's made me a manipulating witch. I don't have a broom nor do I fly but I get around and usually in everyone's business...deep inside I'm miserable so I see to it that everyone is as miserable as me!

• My world's been shaped by my rearing and motivation-less surroundings. I've seen nothing within my reach that would make me yearn for anything other than what I know. I've seen nothing so I want nothing. I've **settled**; in a downward spiral to nowhere just like those around me who've chosen the same. Striving (I think) day by day just to get by... somebody's baby mama, someone's chick on the side, just another man's midnight call...

• I'm **hiding** in disguise, because I don't want to show you who I am. The genuine cover girl layer upon layer – I'm in there somewhere. Although you may not actually be in the closet you've hidden under oversized clothes so that no one can see your frame. Your response, nobody is looking for me; I've been in here a long time, buried under the clothes peeking through the crack in the door to my future. I have no energy to breakthrough; come out, come out wherever you are...

I know why the caged bird sings – silenced and stumped this abuse shut her down as she sought to make sense of what doesn't make sense — Okay, I'll get out of your head.

It's funny that while this book's theme stems from the near assault of sexual abuse, the characteristics of any shaken foundation are all very similar. It doesn't matter whether it is abandonment which steals from one affirmation; mental abuse which kills the ability to dream; love violations that sabotage trust; or any of life's rip-offs that produce the perpetual fight within to avoid the soul's lockdown and the potential for its flight to freedom.

Like Paul and Silas' prison experience, there are people who've prayed for you and the angel of the Lord has come to walk you out of the caged cell that penned you in. He is here right now.

Section 2 – Confrontation: The Staircase

Chapters Five & Six

It is the spring of 2000 at age thirty-nine; I'm in a season of transition as I've come through a near death experience during my pregnancy and the loss of twins. I'm progressing very well as I've learned to be content in whatever state I'm in. Truly, it is well with my soul. Now, in the immediacy of that moment, I clearly had to talk to the Lord because I didn't understand these things. However, in the larger scheme of things, I would soon discover afresh the awesome plan of God for my life. I realized this wasn't just about me as it was about so much more (and so many more). Remember, nothing in our lives take God by surprise, all of our existence is in the course of his handiwork.

One night after our Tuesday Bible Study Fellowship one of the sisters and I went out to get some ice cream at the local ice cream parlor. If you know me, this is one of my favorite past times. I'm famous for special concoctions and enjoyed a heavenly sundae. That evening, I had one of my favorites, a Belgian waffle sundae with vanilla and chocolate soft serve slathered with wet walnuts and butterscotch topping. It was a fun evening. As we went to pay the bill, the sister that was with me asked, "Pastor Tina, do you want some candy…?" In a moment that I have yet to be able to fully articulate, I completely froze. I'm not sure what happened. It felt like a whirlwind shook me where I stood, however this shaking had no motion - real, but not real - an outer body experience. I guess I must have shut down. I don't know how long this took, all I remember is the young lady saying to me, "are you okay, Pastor Tina…are you okay?", this seem to have taken all day. I finally answered her and told her I was fine (I thought), and proceeded to say, "I'll tell you later what going on." As we left the ice cream parlor, I began a mental journey that took me back to Public School 100 in the eerie stairwell where I was offered the candy in exchange for my virtue.

At the cash register counter, the ice cream

parlor sold fresh homemade fudge and other delicacies which included jars of candy that lined the counter top. When I was asked if I wanted some candy, I looked right up at a jar of Now & Laters. I told the young lady, "... remind me to tell you the story of Vanilla Now & Laters".

The exchange of candy for precious treasure was unthinkable; the value not nearly adequate. I rate or attached value to my essence – no one else would ever be given that right. This was a defining moment in my life.

5. Just Like Candy

Life's Imitations

Have you ever been in a dark stairwell, usually the light bulb has been busted and you race to get either to the next level, or out on the next floor? I don't know anyone who likes a dark, enclosed place. It's too much like being entrapped or imprisoned. Even as children we often preferred a nightlight. We'd cry out, 'it's dark in here!', as we panicked until our parents sat with us or turned on a light. Our lives reflect this analogy so as we work through the night times of our journey. Those are the times we are working to settle the tough scenes that our life thrusts us into. Seemingly, we are put into these screen plays without a script. We wing it as we ad lib the required verbiage to get us through the scene and out of the uneasiness we feel.

One of my favorite movies is Imitation of Life. It is the 1959 version of a tear jerker about two women with daughters they we're challenged with. Life's stairwell for them was

5. Just Like Candy

challenging. After frantically searching for her lost daughter Susie at Coney Island, an attractive widow named Lora Meredith finds her playing with Sarah Jane, a light-skinned black girl. Lora then meets Sarah Jane's single black mother, Annie Johnson, and a white photographer named Steve Archer, who takes some photographs of the girls. Lora discovers that Annie and Sarah Jane have no place to go, and although she is poor herself, having come to New York in search of an acting career, she invites the two to stay the night in her small apartment. In exchange for her small room, Annie offers to keep house and look after Susie while Lora seeks acting and modeling jobs. The two women agree to help each other and develop a relationship that spans over years. This sisterhood facilitated a need in both of their complicated lives as they looked out for each other.

One cold day, Annie brings Sarah Jane's galoshes to school, where she discovers that her daughter has been trying to conceal her race from her classmates. When Sarah Jane runs from Annie, her distressed mother turns to Lora and asks, "How do you explain to your child that she was born to be hurt?" What a strange concept adapted by the influence that generation had on this single black woman; 'born to be hurt'…really? **"Man who is born of woman is of few days and full of trouble"**, Job 14:1 speaks to her question as we are all in the same boat; too few days, too many troubles. We need the Lord to navigate our lives as we live in this world.

The story goes on to unfold their often complicated lives as an era of prejudice and indifference shapes their world. Impacted by their reality, we are introduced to these characters and their struggle for survival. The character I most like to address here is Sarah Jane. She is the little, pretty, fair-skinned black girl who wants to be someone that she is not. In one season of her life, Sarah Jane tells Susie that she secretly has been seeing her white boyfriend, and that she would rather die than be considered black. When the young man learns that Sarah Jane's mother is black, however, he beats her. Her quest is the evasive self-denial of all she truly is as she is clueless of what she seeks after and how she ultimately finds her true self love much too late to appreciate it. Sarah Jane's disruptive lifestyle continues as she pursues her false sense of reality at the expense of her inner, personal happiness and the despair of her loving mother whom she despises. This is sad, because so often much of our lack of self importance affects the well being of those around us, especially those we love. Living the lie of wanting to be someone or something that she is not proves to be draining for Sarah Jane. She and Annie have their own struggles, as the light-skinned Sarah Jane is in a constant state of turmoil over her identity and steadfastly wants to pass for white. This distain all started very young for her. Sarah Jane's anger at being black translates into animosity towards her long-suffering mother.

Adolescence has not stopped Sarah Jane from attempting to pass for white: she passes in order to get a job performing at a seedy nightclub, and lies to Annie and tells her she is working at the library. When Annie learns the truth and appears to claim her daughter,

Sarah Jane is fired, and her subsequent dismissal of her mother's care begins taking a physical toll on Annie. Poor Sarah Jane, she's chosen to live in the vicious life of delusion and deceit. The truth is, she deep down inside hates even who she has created herself to be; it's a lose/lose situation.

In another scene, Lora returns from her modeling trip to find that Sarah Jane has run away from home, and has Steve hire a detective to find her. The detective locates Sarah Jane in California, living as a white woman under an assumed name and working as a chorus girl. Annie, becoming weaker and more depressed by the day is convinced she is dying. She decides to fly to California for one last look at her daughter. Sarah Jane is furious, exclaiming, "I'm somebody else, I'm white." Annie then introduces herself to Sarah Jane's white friend as Sarah Jane's former nanny and leaves, but not before Sarah Jane tearfully embraces her. Poor Annie, she is forced to deny love's core value which is truth as she attempts to satisfy the dysfunction of her only child who she loves deeply, yet can not come to terms with and insists she accept who she is. Maybe Annie is challenged with her own introspections.

The two mothers are now alone in the house. One day, Annie tells Lora to make certain all her possessions are left to Sarah Jane and then, after reassuring her old friend that she is "going to glory," dies. Lora breaks down, but sees to it that Annie has the elaborate funeral she had requested. It is here you must get your tissues out; this is a real good rainy, Saturday afternoon tear jerker. All the years of hateful disrespect toward her mother is fueling her awakening as she can no longer hold back the deeply hidden love she actually did have for her. Lora and Susie gently lead her into the hearse, where they reassure her that she did not cause her mother's death. It is a pathetic scene as a remorseful Sarah Jane throws herself upon her mother's casket, begging forgiveness. This scene made me remember those crazy dreams we have when we are running down the stairs and miss several steps as our heart jumps to our stomach and we realize the mad chase was just a bad dream...a nightmare of sorts that we never want to relive. How you fight to grab a hold of something, anything that will prevent you from busting your head open and you wake up to the fact that the safety net is unnecessary. Sadly, all that Sarah Jane wanted was wrapped up in her mother as she was the mirror for her true identity. Until she was comfortable with looking at her in truth, she was never able to be truth to herself. It is at this point that her reality calls her attention to how she came to exist; the mirror image that is now incased in the burial casket.

As per her last wishes, Annie is given a lavish funeral in a large church, complete with a gospel choir led by the great Mahalia Jackson and a parade-like procession with a horse drawn hearse. Lora takes Sarah Jane to their limousine to join her, Suzie, and Steve as the procession slowly travels through the city and the solemn music of the last rites moment is played. The story ends as we hope they will all go on to sweeten the sour candy life has been and turn it for the better. Hopefully, Sarah Jane will get to the place that she chooses to quit being a fake. Her imitation of life has to this point produced no positive, lasting results. She has exhausted herself working to be something she is not. All of her energy has been put into her disguise and she has yet learned to truly live. Somewhere layered deep in her being is the marvelous creation she is to become yet, doesn't even know; sound familiar. What she must do is decide to be true to her self and begin to develop the awesome gift she is called to be regardless of what society's expectation is. She deserved better and so did her mother. Don't be an imitator, choose to be an initiator and show the world the essence of your great grace. Never shrink to another's expectation or classification of you, and God forbid – don't let anyone define your worth.

The Raggedy Ann Discovery

The fictional character, Raggedy Ann created by writer Johnny Gruelle is full of wonder. The rags to riches story is about a child's playtime discovery of a dismembered doll. It was created in 1915 as a rag doll with red yarn for hair, and was introduced to the public in the 1918 book Raggedy Ann Stories. It was a very successful run which also included the introduction of her brother, Raggedy Andy who dressed in a sailor suit and hat. The story goes like this ...a small girl bursts into her father's art studio, trailing a battered rag doll behind her. Panting, she tells Daddy about discovering the faceless doll in Grandmother's attic. Laying aside his afternoon's cartoon, the father picks up the doll. He studies her face for a moment before picking up his cartooning pen and deftly applying a new, whimsical face. He suggests that Grandmother might be enlisted to sew on another shoe button to take care of a missing eye. Then, reaching for a volume of poetry behind his desk, the father browses through several by poet and family friend, James Whitcomb Riley. Compressing the titles of two of his favorites – "The Raggedy Man" and "Little Orphan Annie" — he asks his daughter, "What if we call your new doll Raggedy Ann?"

Out of the dark, obscure treasure store of her grandmother's attic this little girl finds a hidden treasure. She presents it to her father who adds identity to the rag doll as she is faceless. Together, they bring to life this no face, no name, and no purpose plaything that evolves into this young girl's toy. I'm fascinated by this story as it shows me the importance of taking a bad situation and turning it into a good one. From the dark, cold, and hidden crevices of the upstairs storage closet, a little girl finds a potential treasure. Disfigured, she seeks out help to bring life to her discovery and her father helps her paint a face on her new friend. She is further assisted as her playmate receives a shoe button for an eye so that she can see her new companion. Vision is offered to her as her life takes on a new dimension. Out of the attic of this rag dolls despair a legend is born.

I'm convinced we must all paint our own face. We cannot give this pen or brush to anyone else – we are responsible for our own identity. This story mimics our lives as we've all played with dolls. Some of my earliest memories are tied to the fun I've had with my life sized doll babies as I fantasized about new friends, new adventures, and new places. We lived through them as we put on what we wanted to be, using them as an extension of ourselves; our child's play. In my mind, this is how we began to paint our own face as we imagined it to be through the dolls we played with. I believe it is a lesson in futility, as we too can take this principle and apply them to the genuine life application of our personal development. I also remember the Colorform© peel and stick doll forms we used to dress and transform according to our personal whims creating for them life and friendships. And we cannot forget the long living Barbie and Friends that have span generations. This is the 5oth birthday of the Barbie doll and she has covered every aspect of our evolution as young girls and women. You can now go to some toy stores and computer design your own personal Barbie; face and all. They are the soap operas of creative child play for every young girl. So many of us played out our daydreams with the assistance of our favorite dolls and we still hold fond memories of those years.

We are no different than this young girl who too developed her world around the day-in day-out experience of child play, such that much of her dad's writings for the Raggedy Ann Stories were centered around his observation of his own daughter's playtime. By the way, her name was Marcella Delight; what an awesome name. This real-life daughter had an indelible influence on her father's life and career. From serving as his model for his literary protagonist, Marcella, to being his reason for creating his Raggedy Ann in the first place, Marcella was her father's muse. However marred Raggedy Ann's life may have been she was lovingly brought to life again.

You are released to etch your own destiny. We learn this truth from this famous rag doll. Having been left to remain fragmented in the dark and obscure place does not mean this is our lot in life. Our disposition must not be the position we take. We must crave the illumination of the light. Each of us can take the scalpel to our own life and carve out the future we hope for. Our heavenly Father has declared His Will for us in Jeremiah 29:11, **"For I**

know the plans I have for you," declares the LORD, "plans to prosper you and not to harm you, plans to give you hope and a future." None of us has to accept whatever is thrown at us. Our personal predicament does not have to be the position we remain in. Each of us must determine whether or not we are going to fulfill the Lord's plan for our life. We've got to know in our knower that His plans for us are attainable - regardless of what our lot in life has been.

Sadly, Marcella died at age 13 after being vaccinated at school for smallpox without her parents' consent. Authorities blamed a heart defect, but her parents blamed the vaccination. Her father, Mr. Gruelle became an opponent of vaccination, and the Raggedy Ann doll was used as a symbol by the anti-vaccination movement. Raggedy Ann is sometimes used by national sororities as a mascot: the current incarnation of Delta Gamma's official mascot, the Hannah Doll is a Raggedy Ann doll, and Ann also is one of the unofficial mascots of the Alpha Sigma Alpha sorority. Isn't it interesting how this rag to riches journey of the legendary Raggedy Ann mirrors our own journey from darkness to light? How wonderful it is that even from this young girl's short life she left the legacy of innocent child play in the person of this timeless rag doll. Here's another life lesson we can adopt, plan to leave your mark in life; don't leave it up to anyone else to assure that everyone knows you were here in the room of life's existence. Seek to shout from the highest mountain as the earth awaits the arrival of your pure essence. Your presentation to the larger scheme of God cannot be duplicated by anyone else on earth. You are the purest expression of you that there is…, life is not life until your flavor's been added. I am so grateful that God made us all unique and individual. Throughout the ages there is no one person who shares another's fingerprint. You are one of a kind so celebrate the solitary wind of your God-given breeze.

Mrs. Gump's Wisdom

"Life is like a box of chocolates you never know what you're going to get"…this is the famous quote from Tom Hanks as he played the retarded man in the movie, Forrest Gump. His mother taught him many life lessons and to her credit, he lived a fruitful life, in spite of his disability. What she told him is so true; life is what you make it. It really is like the mystery of biting into a piece of chocolate thinking it's cherry-filled and winding up with a peanut. Now peanuts are good if you like them, the point being – you've got to make the best of what you get to work with. "You got to do the best with what God gave you", Mrs. Gump (smart lady). You've heard the saying, if life gives you a bunch of lemons make lemonade. In all purity, the best things in life are the simple lessons that fold into who we each become. Sometimes they are learned the hard way, however once the lesson is learned it produces a new stability we can then build upon. Life is a series of these types of lessons and applications. There are times we have to shelf some of them as we are not prepared to receive them during certain seasons of our lives. We have to avoid forgetting where we've placed these inconvenient lessons until we grow up and are ready to handle what we had to shelf. Again, all of life is relative. That's what I like about Forrest Gump's character; he made the pure best of what he had to work with, no excuses. He produced in his day and lived out a meaningful life without regard to his mental challenge. Each of us may take some hard hits over the course of life but we don't have to fall down every time. If we do we need to get back up again. One of the famous beatitudes states, **"Blessed are the pure in heart, for they shall see God"**, Matthew 5:8.

As life happens to each of us, there are various responses we have to the occurrences each day may bring. We have all learned that there are some things in life we can do nothing about and yet others that are clearly within our control. The great balancing act is to sift through the stuff and pull out that which will assist us with a healthy life perspective. How we view our life's cycles based on this perspective will usually set our position on it. This is challenging because all things are pure to the pure. So if my life has been impacted by defilement, my life view is affected by them.

We are the sum total of all of our experiences. This is why it is so important to sort out the good, the bad, and the indifferent so that we can properly access what should be done with it all. I've got to guard my heart as the scripture says because out of it flows the issues of life [Proverbs 4:23]. Life is filled with issues. I must wrestle my life to pin down the stuff that will cloud my eye-view. The clearer I see the better my view; the better my view, the fuller my scope for success. This begins with being truthful with the confrontation with life itself – my life. It starts with an introspection of your inner parts. It is here where you can not lie; it is what it is! When I've settled it all in the inner part I'm on the road to a better me.

"Surely you desire truth in the inner parts; you teach me wisdom in the inmost place. Create in me a pure heart, O God, and renew a steadfast spirit within me. Do not cast me from your presence or take your Holy Spirit from me. Restore to me the joy of your salvation and grant me a willing spirit, to sustain

me", Psalms 51:6; 10-12. This was David's cry as he sought to relieve himself from his inner despair. The Lord is our helper in this pursuit for fierce purity. He is after truth from the inside out. His wisdom shoots down all of our rationalization as it sets the standard we judge our life by. There's no argument here or at least not one you can win. God always tells the truth. My willingness to submit to this continual process of review is what sustains me for successful living. It is only now that I begin to walk in the more pure and perfect way as I am guided by the life truths that apply to the personal blueprint God drew out for me.

"To the pure, all things are pure, but to those who are corrupted and do not believe, nothing is pure. In fact, both their minds and consciences are corrupted", Titus 1:15. The will of God for our lives is peace, to settle for anything less than that is our bad choice. We do good to regularly go over the check list of our lives. One event does not necessarily depend upon another. God's ultimate purpose for us cannot be destroyed by others. His purpose is more internal than it is external. The Lord desires that we each become the internal person that he wants us to be – a person of character. Do not become an outward success but an inward failure. "Don't be an outward show to a wicked world", my grandfather, Ernest Solomon used to say. What sense does it make to "show off" to a misguided world? Why not show them who they can emulate? Our actions must line up with our words. All of life has been fighting against us becoming who we are destined to be so we have to decide to kick back.

Each of us must be reintroduced and developed into the full stature of our God-given style and finesse. The world will miss your special impression if you don't show up. The sweet mystery of our femininity is a journey we must intentionally embrace. We can't remain accustomed to mediocrity and the basic instinct to live in the status quo, fulfilling the myths and stereotypes society has placed upon us. The stereotypical view of African-American women as sex objects through the historical roots of slavery is an area we must overcome. We must combat the negative myths and stereotypes that still affect women of all kinds, especially black women. A thought-provoking dialogue is a good beginning to expose this misdirection. Every woman must realize she is a treasure, the valuation of her worth was determined by God, and prior to Adam's awakening, God had fashioned a diamond. If we fail to see and understand this, we will disregard and discard our worth and so will everyone else we come in contact with. You must now show up!

We need to begin to pray that God will help us to reclaim our innocence. His original plan began in purity. It is a virtue worth fighting for as it sustains our unique offering to mankind.

Candy is good but too much of it, rots your teeth, is bad for sugar, and it causes us to gain weight. We've got to monitor the sweets. In the Song of Songs, the poet writes, **"Daughters of Jerusalem, I charge you: Do not arouse or awaken love until it so desires"** (8:4). One paraphrase of this statement can be as follows: **"Do not awaken sex-**

ual passion before you are in a position to lawfully give way to its full expression." We deserve God's finest. If we arouse sexual desires prematurely we rob ourselves. In the case of assault, we must work especially harder to reclaim our innocence. Once awakened, a Pandora's Box of unwanted problems is presented. Often we are unprepared for the emotional attention they need as we are challenged with new moral issues that can remain our continual struggle for most of our life. Fully developed does not mean ready to operate. There's a transition in Forest Gump's life that he too had to make the adjustment in response to his sexuality. When he and Jenny got together, we see the instance where his emotional stability is impacted by his physical reality. Left to himself and largely unaware of the significance of their intimacy, he had to process the flood of emotion that this encounter presented. There is an emotional preparedness that should also accompany physical development. Many of us were never prepared through the matriculation toward the full expression of sexual intimacy. We were prematurely introduced to sexuality. This is why it is so important to renew our mind to the will of God and redirect our thinking with the mind of Christ. Paul said it like this to the church at Corinth when he encouraged them not to act like children, **"Brethren, do not be children in your thinking; yet in evil be babes, but in your thinking be mature"** 1 Corinthians 14:20 NAS. You're a big girl now and yet you are still Daddy's little girl. You must ask yourself, "Am I truly ready for this?" Our heavenly Father has plans for our lives that our eyes have not seen.

We were born with a precious innocence, a childlike grace which is a gift from God. Ideally, as we grow and develop we are ever adding onto this innocence, virtue. Some woman may be sexually innocent, not because they are pure in heart, but simply because they have not been tested in the area of moral excellence. Just because one is a virgin it does not mean that their thoughts are pure. They likely have not played out the thoughts that are in their heart. So, what does it mean to be pure in heart? Purity of heart has to do with the hidden motives and intentions of the heart. The things we think about and do when nobody is around to hold us accountable. We know ourselves best, if given opportunity we too may give way to sin if it presents itself. Though we never fully know our hearts, because it is, **"deceitful above all things and beyond cure"** Jeremiah 17:9, we must daily expose our hearts to the Word of God and the on-going work of the Holy Spirit. Don't let your own heart fool or fail you! Because the human heart may have secret areas of rebellion not yet exposed by the fires of temptation, every sincere Christian must pray, **"Search me, O God, and know my heart; test me and know my anxious thoughts. See if there is any offensive way in me, and lead me in the way everlasting"** Psalms 139:23-24 NKJV.

In this respect, one becomes virtuous not by virtue of being shielded from sin, but by purposefully seeking to know God's heart as it relates to individual purity and by actively seeking to live accordingly. On the other hand, if you've had a past history of sexual/

moral failure you must intentionally choose to live a Spirit-directed life concerning sexual purity and emotional wholeness. It is imperative that we attain the same standard of virtue in the eyes of God! King David did this as he confessed his fault and sin to God in his prayer of Psalms 51 – **"Create in me a clean heart and renew a right spirit within me."** He longed to be present in the presence of God, not simply going through the motions of hidden sins of the heart and body. He learned how to regain his innocence and add virtue to his life as the Lord refers to him as a man after His own heart. He sought God on a level that helped him to restore his position and relationship with the Lord. Virtue in its 'finest form' is simply this: to know evil yet to purposefully choose that which is good. Thankfully there are none of us who are without hope because as we turn to the cross of Jesus Christ, it is there that we find our common denominator; each of us stands on level ground. Virgins and those who are sexually experienced on all levels, stand on equal footing through the cleansing blood of Christ!

David's counterpart is another prime example of this - Bathsheba went from moral defeat to a Woman of Virtue. She too didn't waste her days dwelling on her splattered past. She walked in the provision of God and found His will for her life. Her legacy more greatly includes the memorial of her name in the canon of biblical history, indirectly in the genealogy of Jesus Christ [Matthew 1:6] – not as David's mistress alone.

6. There's a Way About a Woman

Mothers and Grandmothers

The Bible declares that the older women should teach the younger women [Titus 2]. There was a day when this was the norm in our culture. The strength of our existence is built on the shoulders of women who got it. We represent a lineage of strong, confident, women who proved that there is an overcomer in each of us. In their simple terms, they displayed life on a level many of us grapple to comprehend. I've found that this is true across cultures as there appears to be an innate strength in the female that speaks volumes without ever saying a word. They had the ability to work through pain and strain without complaint. It has proven their resilience. They imparted this grace into us and empower us with the lessons their legacies left for our perusal.

My grandmother Elizabeth wasn't an educated woman but she could pray like I've heard no one else. She also had a really funny side to her as she'd do the camel walk and drop her hip as we watched her move - when she danced it looked like glitter. She was a fascinating woman, whose wisdom and depth exuded in very practical ways. My mother in law, Millicent was pure brilliance as she pulled most anything together with her special flair. She had a knack for creativity and innovation that very few possess. They embodied a sassy, sensuality that was ever so pure. It made you smile about womanhood. In the routine day-to day things they did, as well as the lessons they taught. My dear mother, Agnes who I'd sit in the kitchen with was a cook extraordinaire. She flavored life with this unique expression even while she cooked; she'd say things like, "everything's better with a little sugar..." She emitted a fanciful aura in all she did. I'm convinced there was something special in her hand. She also stamped an indelible image in our hearts of the best of femininity, seemingly with little effort; we are branded forever. The pizzazz of my grandmother Earlene's 'sock-it-to-me' cake is like no other I've tasted. Her life mimics the triumph over an early start in life with the responsibility of a young child in an era when it wasn't the norm. I also remember a visit at her house and my great-grandmother, Sally was there – she was an intriguing woman. In my child's eye this very tall, caramel lady sat strong like an Indian chief in the western movies I'd seen. Her two long braids seem to sit right in the wing-backed chair on either side of her hips as I stared at her in amazement – our very own Pocahontas. She exuded firm strength and a glowing grace. Then there's Florence-Mama who dropped golden nuggets of womanly wisdom when she shared her heart and told me how she'd regretted taking her teaching job miles away as she was a newlywed girl. It was a miracle that she had gone to Teacher's College during the early '30's there in South Carolina – but her young marriage and new motherhood didn't sustain the distance. As she said, "I was too far away". She was a class act. Ironically, she called me her little Pocahontas..., I loved our little talks. These women left a trail of simple grace that my mind recalls fondly as the golden dust and wonder of Wisdom Was. Over time we've moved away from this maternal impartation of strong godly influencers who didn't take tea for the fever. That's why I call them "Wisdom Was". They spoke to us in an evasive language that cut to the chase of our reality and clearly put things in perspective. Wisdom Was..., was in your face with truth and undeniable persistence that required your ear and attention. They didn't play with us. No one got away from their piercing stare; firm embrace; or bull horn speech that sent tremors to our soul. Although they referred to our sexuality in terms unidentifiable, they made no bones about how we were to conduct ourselves as godly young women.

Wisdom Was is that cloud of solid witnesses we rely on when we reflect on the strength of our mothers, grandmothers, aunts, and sisters who did life well. The things we accept today, they cried over in years past. We owe it to their legacy to never fail or diminish their influence by not maintaining the standard they set. They chuckled at our feeble attempts at love as they taught us to honor our heart when they said, "Girl, you are better (or deserve better) than that..." And although we often failed to listen we knew they were telling the truth.

One of the most prolific teachers of our time is a woman named, Dr. Maya Angelou. She is heralded around the world for her insight and depth of wisdom, particularly about womanhood. This is one of my favorite quotes from her, "Becoming an old female may require only being born with certain genitalia, inheriting long-living genes and the fortune not to be run over by an out of control truck...". Our chances at becoming something more than an old female are slim to none if we aren't intentionally prepare to. We have to apply some common sense attention to the development of who we are. We need a plan of action. In her poem, And Still I Rise..., Dr. Angelou presents the undeniable and unbreakable strength and spirit of the African American people, past and present. There's a portion where she identifies the grace and innate celebration of the mystery of our God-given purity. In it she cites,

- Does My sexiness upset you
- Does it come as a surprise

6. There's a Way About a Woman

- That I dance like I've got diamonds
- At the meeting of my thighs?

Could this be like those diamonds in the rough? The stuff we forfeit at the expense of our not knowing or acting like we know any better. The same old - same old will no longer work for us, we need a God Plan to help us understand this marvelous mystery that is so much of our being and not solely operate from the waist down. Our emotional well being is woven into the fabric of our purity and thereby, our sexuality. Our physical strength is also impacted by it. We must learn to celebrate the whole of our being and begin to function from an intelligent, head down position. You better think...think about what's really important. Don't check your brain at the door of life! The fact is, my sexuality does not stem from my vagina; the heart is where my sexually begins. Until I decide in my heart what I want out of my life at every level, I'm one miserable soul.

Sexuality has been regulated to the yearning in our loins at the expense of our heart. In the words of the Shulamite woman we too must declare that I am my beloved and he is mine – his banner over me is love. Look at these special words from Song of Solomon 4:12 and 16, [verse 12] **"You are a garden locked up, my sister, my bride; you are a spring enclosed, a sealed fountain."** [Verse 16] **"Awake, north wind, and come, south wind! Blow on my garden that its fragrance may spread abroad. Let my lover come into his garden and taste its choice fruits."** This is heart to heart talk by covenant lovers, not just loins or sexual organs offering suggestions. What she and her beloved knew was pure. It was truly satisfying. They engaged at a level that only enhanced their physical celebration and exchange.

As we look back at Esther, this young virgin had no point of reference for what her presentation would mean to the king, let alone the joy that covenant oneness would bring. She too tapped into this mystery; covenant love that fuses two hearts. As she was trained over that year long period, she was taught many things. She also had the opportunity to observe her surroundings and learn from her exchanges with the other women. In addition to this, she was mentored by Hegai, the king's eunuch, who was in charge of the women as they received instruction and regular beauty treatments [Esther 2:3-4]. The Bible says that Esther was lovely in form and features. The girl pleased him and won his favor. Immediately he provided her with her beauty treatments and special food. He assigned to her seven maids selected from the king's palace and moved her and her maids into the best place in the harem. Esther didn't have to "put it on"; she seemed to have something special that didn't require the fluff or extra layers we tend to add. He was enamored with her beauty. That special something was the outflow from her heart purity that perfected her wholeness; the king hadn't seen anything like it. It knocked him off his feet.

She went through a preparation period. The process required that before a girl's turn came to go in to King Xerxes, she had to complete twelve months of beauty treatments prescribed for the women, six months with oil of myrrh and six with perfumes and cosmetics.

There is a Jewish rite that is similar to this preparation process. It embodies what is called the Mikvah. In the beginning there was only water (which represents purity). A miraculous compound, it is the primary source and vivifying factor of all sustenance and, by extension, all life as we know it. But Judaism teaches it is more. For these very same attributes — water as source and sustaining energy — are mirrored in the spiritual. Water has the power to purify: to restore and replenish life to our essential, spiritual selves.

The mikvah personifies both the womb and the grave; the portals to life and afterlife. In both, the person is stripped of all power and prowess. In both there is a mode of total reliance, complete resignation of control. The mikvah is a bath or pool of cleansing water – to me it represents the ritual of routine... consistency. It reminds me of the things we gloss over in the course of living that truly have weighty value.

Immersion in the mikvah can be understood as a symbolic act of self-denial, the conscious suspension of the self as an autonomous force. In so doing, the immersing Jew signals a desire to achieve oneness with the source of all life, to return to a primeval unity with God. Immersion indicates the abandonment of one form of existence to embrace one infinitely higher – this is also the premise for our baptism. In other words there is an abandonment of what previously existed to embrace the hope of what can be. In keeping with this theme, immersion in the mikvah is described not only in terms of purification, revitalization, and rejuvenation but also — and perhaps primarily — as rebirth.

In years gone by, menstruating women were a grave source of awe and fear. At best they were avoided, at worst they were shunned and cast aside. Often, menstruating women were blamed for tragedy and mishap, as if they had polluted the environment with their breath or gaze. This was a simplistic, if not misguided, response to a complex phenomenon whose rhyme and reason eluded the primitive mind. In those societies, peace could be made with menstruation only by ascribing it to evil and demonic spirits and by the adaptation of a social structure that facilitated its avoidance.

Viewed against this backdrop, the Jewish rhythm (birth control) in marriage is perceived by many as a throwback to archaic taboos, a system rooted in antiquated attitudes and a widespread form of hatred of women. For the Jew, family purity is a celebration of life and our most precious human relationships. It can be understood most fully only within a deeper notion of purity and impurity.

Judaism teaches that the source of all taharah, "purity," is life itself. Conversely, death is the harbinger of tumah, "impurity." All types of ritual impurity, and the Torah describes many, are rooted in the absence of life or some measure - even a whisper - of death.

When stripped to its essence, a woman's menses signals the death of potential life. Each month a woman's body prepares for the possibility of conception. The uterine lining is built up — rich and replete, ready to serve as a cradle for life — in anticipation of a fertilized ovum. Menstruation is the shedding of the lining, the end of this possibility.

6. There's a Way About a Woman

The presence of potential life within fills a woman's body with holiness and purity. With the departure of this potential, impurity sets in, conferring upon the woman a state of impurity or, more specifically, niddut. Impurity is neither evil nor dangerous and it is not something tangible. Impurity is a spiritual state of being, the absence of purity, much as darkness is the absence of light. Only immersion in the mikvah, following the requisite preparation, has the power to change the status of the woman.

The concept of purity and impurity as mandated by the Torah and applied within Jewish life is unique; it has no parallel or equivalent in this postmodern age. Perhaps that is why it is difficult for the contemporary mind to relate to the notion and view it as relevant.

A mikvah is a pool of water used for a variety of purification rituals:

• Married women immerse at the end of seven days from the end of each monthly menstrual cycle, in preparation for the resumption of marital relations.

• Brides, and bridegrooms, immerse

themselves in preparation for their wedding.

• Immersion is required for gentiles who wish to become a Jew.

• Men go to the mikvah the day before Yom Kippur, and in some communities prior to Shabbat and festivals.

• New dishes and utensils are immersed prior to using.

This purification is a shadow of Water Baptism; the contemporary in the Old Testament is the Red Sea, and in the New Testament, it is John's baptism in the Jordan. A woman's preparation entailed much of this as she is fully immersed under the cleansing water. It has presently been reintroduced into the Jewish culture and is the special celebration rite one visits the Temple for on a monthly basis.

And this is how Esther went to the king after her year-long preparation: anything she wanted was given her to take with her from the harem to the king's palace. In the evening she would go there and in the morning return to another part of the harem to the care of Shaashgaz, the king's eunuch who was in charge of the concubines. She would not return to the king unless he was pleased with her and summoned her by name. When the turn came for Esther to go to the king, she asked for nothing other than what Hegai, the king's eunuch who was in charge of the harem, suggested. And Esther won the favor of everyone who saw her. Now I know what you're saying, what does this have to do with Titus 2 women? While Esther's instructors were the king's eunuchs and her guardian Mordecai, she was teachable and receptive to the impartation of those who helped develop her for womanhood. She learned to celebrate the season of her purification. We must begin to cry out again for our mothers, those influencers, and models who've set the course before us; those who challenged us to walk the more perfect way. Most importantly, we must be open to their wisdom and apply their instruction. Remember, you didn't go through just for you. Your pathway in life is to prepare you to assist others as we benefit from those things that help us to overcome. We must also begin to embody the very essence of the "star" that each of us is, like Esther. Her feeble beginning, through the providence of God, brought deliverance to a whole nation.

Consider this, what did Esther learn? What secrets was she given? What made the king's heart skip a beat? Sex, (good or bad) comes a dime a dozen, but very few have ever made love! This is the purity we long for. We can learn a strong lesson from this. Let's be honest ladies, we've regulated our sexuality to the yearning in our loins at the expense of our heart. The repeated cycle of bad relationship after sad relationship is proof of this. Spurts of joy have shortened the lasting moments we have longed for as we've taken whatever came our way. The fizzled out memories are not even worth reviewing; they're more like a series of bad dreams. This young virgin can help us review our life from the insight of her innocence. Ideally, this should be our case but it is often not. Minding her business, she is summoned to the king's court as he is seeking a new wife. She is among the company of several young ladies vying for his attention. However, she stands above all the rest. The preparations in her heart are what I believe won her favor with the king. We've missed it. There is something a man wants to see that has nothing to do with what we've been displaying. While they are visual by nature, there is more than what meets the eye that opens up your mystery. It's a heart issue that even they can't explain but they know its strength when it is revealed to them. But we've got to secure it first and be careful who we give this treasure to. Esther learned some stuff. Those secrets enabled her to secure her position as she won the king's heart and made it shift its beat. She tapped into her rhythm and synchronized his to pure oneness; he didn't get "that" from the others.

Here is another example of what I call a "this was for that moment"; it's the review or reflection of the things that seem to come together which previously didn't make any sense. It's generally a change of attitude or perspective that jars your memory and causes you to reconsider the potential benefit of another time or season in your life, regardless of how negative or positive it may have been. It's like your wake up moment where you stretch out and decide to take on the world because you feel you have mastered a serious life lesson or experience. Each of us will have a different encounter in our moments of preparedness. I call it "Primetime", the curtain is raised and the show must go on. It is what we've been working on all along, but sometimes didn't realize or appreciate that moment's significance. It is the Why, when she chooses to identify herself.

In this age, our culture has embraced the sexual revolution and anything goes. We've even been bombarded in the church where we've accepted the course that society has set. Where are the sisters that will declare that the buck stops here and reset the direction to a wholesome, godly celebration of the glorious grace of our femininity? Is there anybody out here who still believes God? There is a pressing need for forward progress; however without a God-inspired purpose we will continue to suffer the abuse of one of God's greatest gifts in our sexuality. This is a part of the continual assault on the purity of our feminine being. The longer we keep living these lies, the harder it will be to break free from there clinches. If it feels good do it, bottoms out as it can only satisfy the temporary "feeling" associated with a one-sided joy of life at the expense of our personal fulfillment. I hear you talking to me, 'well, that's enough for right now – I'll just get by with this'. My response to you is, "will you?" How long will you be someone's diversion without any meaningful commitment? Why have we, even in the church accepted this ungodly set of society's view? Where is our heart's hope in all this chaos? Don't you want the Father's best?

We are not much different than the spiritual condition which described the church at Laodicea. In the Book of Revelation the Holy Spirit's message to them was a stern warning. Their condition was diagnosed as being spiritually lukewarm and worldly. It produced a professing church that was rich, cultured, and religiously ritualistic. They were so self-satisfied and carnal that their empathy tossed out any semblance of Christ's authority in their lives. He is represented prophetically as standing on the outside knocking for admission [Revelation 3:20]. No longer is He admitted by the corporate body, but stands outside extending an invitation to individuals. How despicable we too have become as we've chosen to live with reckless abandonment when the Truth has been made available to us. This awful spiritual condition is so utterly abhorrent to God. He would rather we be hot or cold; in or out; light or darkness; as he states, **"So because you are lukewarm, and neither hot nor cold, I will spit you out of My mouth"**, Revelation 3:16. Church girls... what are we doing? My precious sisters why aren't we thinking? Single women, can you afford this reckless path of living in a day filled with such dire consequences? What can truly fill our hearts void?

Those who are licensed don't want to make love and those who are not, are having all the sex they want. Married folks hide behind their familiarity with each other refusing to do what's necessary to keep the marriage flame burning. The unmarried's answer to this is that we're grown and we all have needs. We sisters have become pathetic as we complain about what we tolerate. Where is the strength that taught us to fight for what is good for us? Is this the best we can offer ourselves? You see, your happiness is your responsibility. Don't sell your soul short! We are all equipped with the gifts and the anointing that ignite marital joy, however it is just that; confined to our covenant oneness. We must affirm our sexuality. Where are the sisters that will declare that we will draw the line in the sand and reset the direction to a wholesome, godly celebration of the glorious grace of our femininity and stop walking around giving headship authority of our lives to every Tom, Dick, and Harry that comes along? Can this man truly walk with me toward God's finest in my life (in our lives)? If not, why waste your time with him? God knows they are not even worth the time we've spent trying to make something fruitful out of these relations. We must take responsibility to make the right choice(s) again. After we review our course, we must reevaluate where we are and where we plan to be. It is high time for the Woman of God to blaze the trails and to set the standard for godly living. We must again, define, by the Word, the position of womankind here in the earth. We can not hide behind the smoke screen of indifference. How is the world to see our Father's heart if we don't display it in all purity? How dare you live beneath your privilege and high call as a Woman of God! Stand fast in the liberty wherein Christ has made you free. We must now take personal responsibility to set the estimate or value of our personal worth and rate our stature in the scheme of God. We must agree with His declaration of who we are. Now here's where the rubber meets the road. We have to decide to agree with God against the grain of what we have been accustomed to and it is not easy. **"It is God's will that you should be sanctified: that you should avoid sexual immorality; that each of you should learn to control his own body in a way that is holy and honorable, not in passionate lust like the heathen, who do not know God; and that in this matter no one**

should wrong his brother or take advantage of him. The Lord will punish men for all such sins, as we have already told you and warned you. For God did not call us to be impure, but to live a holy life." 1 Thessalonians 4:3-7, NIV.

God wants us to live a pure life. We've got to relearn to appreciate and give dignity to our body, not abuse it. God hasn't invited us into a disorderly, unkempt life but to a beautiful one – displayed from the inside out. Your brother is your brother until he is your husband; don't run roughshod over each other in this matter. You deserve better and so does God. I know this is a bold position to take, however it is the sensible one. Am I willing to give myself wholly to this? Here is some help, **"So here's what I want you to do, God helping you: Take your everyday, ordinary life-your sleeping, eating, going-to-work, and walking-around life-and place it before God as an offering. Embracing what God does for you is the best thing you can do for him. Don't become so well adjusted to your culture that you fit into it with-**

out even thinking. Instead, fix your attention on God. You'll be changed from the inside out. Readily recognize what he wants from you, and quickly respond to it. Unlike the culture around you, always dragging you down to its level of immaturity, God brings out the best in you, develops well-formed maturity in you." Romans 12:1 & 2, The Message Bible. You're a big girl, now is a good time to begin to act like it.

Section 3 – The Revelation of the Stairwell's Purpose

The Final Chapter:

It's the winter of '07, the dawn of a new day. At age forty-six I'm in a year of maintenance where I've begun to work on the 10th anniversary edition of Always A Lady. My plan had been to revise the original manuscript with it's fourth printing and include the workbook I'd been teaching from over the years to commemorate the tenth year. Midway in the process I began to get the sense that this was not the way to go. I kept praying and writing but there was a slant on the direction of the text. An illumination of thought began to come together over several observations I had from a group of teaching sessions I'd done. I began to see my life mirrored in the faces of multitudes of women, some I didn't even know. What was so funny is that I saw that there was nothing new under the sun. Although we had come together from different paths, we weren't much different. The pull on my spirit shifted me to a new level of exposure to the depth of inner victory I'd learned to walk in. I further understood what Paul meant when he said he had poured his life out as a drink offering to God. People needed someone to be transparent and say it's not easy, but it is possible to have it all together (nearly). It wasn't until a series of requests were presented to me that I began to truly see what the Lord was doing. I'd been teaching on breakthrough and deliverance and during these sessions, I began to see women of all ages coming into years of long awaited release as the anointing broke entangled yokes. They fought through years of the muck and mire of unresolved challenges. They began to voice their pending deliverance and received strength to bust open their own heart cry. The seed bed of much of this despair was a lifelong struggle for many who had adjusted and adapted to varied levels of dysfunction. Their tainted lives were marred by impurities we were all familiar with. It was easy to show empathy. I revisited my original assignment from God and sat to hear what He wanted to do. I then got a call that confirmed for me that now was the time to go full throttle with the instruction on the purity of our sexuality; the grace of our feminine being and why the assault on its destruction is so fierce - thus, Vanilla Now & Later...a sequel to Always A Lady.

There's a way about a woman. She is indeed a sweet mystery. She is His fascinating creation; an awesome wonder. God fashioned a diamond when He brought her forth. In this hour, He has called forth our authenticity as we are to operate in purity - correctly. If we fail to see and understand this, we will disregard his intention. Again, if we discard our worth, so will everyone else.

7. Dawn of a New Day

D-day (Reckoning, Settlement, and Peace)

This is the Dawn of a New Day and I thank God for his faithfulness, indeed his loving kindness is better than life. It was about five o'clock in the morning and I'm rolling over in my final stages of rest. I was abruptly awakened out of a good sleep because I was cold. As I popped up I realized everything on me was wet. I was having a special lady moment. In the morning dawn, I decided that when I get to heaven I'm going to talk to Eve, as I think I'm getting ready to go through some "pre" something and it's causing me a few challenges. I've got to get up and change the T-shirt I'm wearing and put a towel on the bed (I'm on the road ministering in the Bronx). What's going on here, my whole world is shifting and again I'm not prepared for this. This is too much (I'm thinking), just too much. I switch pillows as I ponder, its tough being a girl..., all these life changes and nothing I can do about them. I'm going to do some research and figure out what I should and should not do to prevent the effects of these changes. I'll ask God what I can do to make it easier because I do not like this battle, not at all. However, I'm so grateful that I'm a girl - I wouldn't want to be anything else but that, I said I wouldn't want to be anything else but a girl. I really mean that. I'm so grateful that God made me female and I'm certainly that. I like to say about myself, I'm a girl amplified; the amplified version with every adjective that describes her. I love being a woman, someone special in the kingdom of God. God has equipped us to be and to become and this excites me nonetheless.

Here we begin to get into the meat of what it is we've been exploring. The reckoning stage sets us up to confront some things that have potentially held us back in a helpless state of passivity. Some of these challenges we've been really working on pressing through, whether trying to make it happen for ourselves individually, or collectively. I believe God that He is actually causing us to shake off, whatever it is that has actually held us and is keeping us in bondage. Let me be clear before we go any further, I'm not talking about the kind of bondage where one is possessed or something, but I'm dealing with the things over the course of our journey that have attached themselves to us. They have blinded us to the abundance that God has for us. The Bible says that the thief comes only to steal, to kill, and to destroy; but our Father has made available life and that life, more abundantly. This abundant life is not just for all your bills to be paid, it is to secure our holistic, everyday life on these mean streets and to avert every plot against our forward progression. It's a new day. That's right, today you can actually have a peace about what it is that you are doing and even on your bad day or in the bad situations you can walk in the peace of God. This is what He wants us to enjoy, not the cloudy days of our past, filled with bad memories or thoughts of times gone by. The "if I would have...wish I should have" days are gone with all their regrets; it's time to move on. Actually, what we do a lot of times or need to do is reflect back and see the lessons that we learned in seasons that we call despair or dysfunction and build on that as opposed to live there. I must gain an appreciation for the seasons of my female journey and accept what I cannot change. Believe me - our diligence in this arena will pay off.

The Awakening

I've found there are too many of us are living in what it was that we did or didn't do and we find it difficult to move on. Now we want to move forward from here, however tough it is. It is high time to address a lot of this stuff as we chop it up on the wood block and walk out the liberty that God has for us. In Romans 7:21-23 the word declares, **"It seems to be a fact of life that when I want to do what is right, I inevitably do what is wrong. I love to do God's will so far as my new nature is concerned; but there is something else deep within me, in my lower nature, that is at war with my mind and wins the fight and makes me a slave to the sin that is still within**

me. In my mind I want to be God's willing servant, but instead I find myself
still enslaved to sin. So you see how it is:
my new life tells me to do right, but the
old nature that is still inside me loves
to sin. Oh, what a terrible predicament
I'm in! Who will free me from my slavery to this deadly lower nature? Thank
God! It has been done by Jesus Christ
our Lord. He has set me free." [TLB] It is
ironic; I've found that death is often a powerful awakening. There is one of two components here that Paul is speaking about which
help us to come to grips with what our heart
may be struggling with. There are actually
three components: the first one is in verse 22
where it refers to us delighting in the law of
God according to the inward man, the next
verse says that he finds another law working
in his members warring against the law in his
mind, these two contrast each other. When he
makes reference here to this law he speaks
of the fight in his soul realm, which is in his
mind. His soul loves Jesus, but he finds this
other component that works against that love.

7. Dawn of a New Day

In my mind I want to do right, but there's a pull against my soul. I know here in my head what I should do in this instance, I know here what I should do in this situation, and I know here what course I should take with this particular incident or relationship. I know here in my head what the right thing to do is, but processing all of the other elements of the decision is the problem. In my whole being is generally where I get the challenge, this is what Paul is speaking about the law in my members and the law in my mind is contrary to one another, and it is there where we fight and struggle to stay on course with God. It's a never ending battle. Finally, he says I know to do good, but my members are subject to the condition(s) that I'm in and the people I'm around. In addition to this, the circumstances that I submit to, whatever they are, either end or facilitate the conflict. He then makes this statement, which is the third component, its in verse 24; it is each of our cry at any given stage of our life. He says here, **"Oh wretched man that I am, WHO can deliver me from this body of death..."** and that's key right there, because can't nobody do it for us but Jesus, and no one can do it like Him either. The punishment of this body of death was that the captive had to carry it around as it decayed upon his back. The stench and weight was the strength of the punishment, but praise God He has delivered us from the body of death. How would you feel with all of this weight on you? This is what out past feels like when we fail to walk in liberty. This body of death is like the hard drive of a computer, although you delete the memory it can still be pulled up from the trash. What a powerful analogy because what we thought we gave up or were done with can be retrieved again, but in God it's very different. Don't fall back to your familiar bend! This is our New Day, what we release goes into the Sea of Forgetfulness never to be reviewed again. Although it goes in the trashcan I don't want you to pick it up again so let's quit spending time there. The victory walk here, is to get in agreement with what I will to do (which is what God wants), and what I want to do. We can't settle for anything less. Like Paul, I get up every morning and I mortify (crush) the deeds of my flesh so that I can help my spirit man with the war between my mind and members. It is only then that I begin to balance out my "would do" and my "want to" which produces a life of purity and peace of mind.

It Is What It Is...

Heavenly Father, You are the one who validates us and gives us authenticity. God designed sex from the very beginning and He called everything He made good. He never set a standard for the male and another for the female. He presented sex in the purity that it is. We've faltered in that we called it okay for a man to "sow his wild oats" and awarded him for his adventures. This was not in God original intent. Unfortunately our brothers have also been deceived by this myth; thereby we've produced men who are also confused in their sexuality. It's as if God is still asking, **"Adam, where are you?"**

When God created Adam and Eve they were naked and not ashamed. As they were presented to each other, they joined together in pure sexual fellowship. Needless to say, after the fall they lost their innocence and began a downward spiral which includes the perversion of God's original intention for their pure relationship. Do you recall God's question to Adam… **"Who told you that you were naked"?** Innocence is the gift they were given, but purity is a process. We must seize this opportunity to regain our place in purity as God reminds us of the gift of innocence. He is calling us afresh and wants our lives to become a sweet smelling savor of worship to Him. His hope in us is a full functioning of every useful expression of our precious "feminine" being. We are a glorious celebration of all that His wondrous creation in us enfolds. There is that special moment in a woman's life that she has prepared for over the course of her journey. It is the juncture where she awakens to her valuable worth as she is affirmed by her Heavenly Father. From her quest to search for her place of significance, she emerges from obscurity to her own, liberating spotlight; it is much like Queen Esther…from her very own private preparation to her glorious public presentation. All of who she is and what she embodies is balanced out for her divine inaugural. It is here that she learns to make no apology for the grace of her femininity. The curtain is raised and we too are being presented at center stage to display God's original intent for the female creation. He fashioned this glorious fusion of feminine grace and the earth is crying out for its display. Who knows my sister, whether you have been called to the Kingdom for such a time as this?

Epilogue: Open Your Heart To The Next Level

There is a woman in the Bible who was a prosperous businesswoman of the city of Thyatira, her name is Lydia. She was one of the first European converts of Paul's ministry in the Asia Minor region. The backdrop of her story is that she was a powerful proselyte intercessor. Prior to her conversion, it appears she carried out a fairly successful life however, she didn't know God. I'm sure this void in her life also looked like an up hill battle. From the bottom of the stairs life looks like a difficult climb when one is void of hope. The risers that represent our progression strain our muscles as we lift ourselves in upward progress. It takes a lot of effort to make the necessary moves that take us from one level to the next. Each step gives us the advantage we need to see clearer the top of the stairs. Its funny how in order to avoid getting tripped up we are required to look down to assure our footing. It sometimes helps to look back too. However difficult the pain of the bump on your knee from the fall up or down the stairs, it pays to review what may help to avoid it. The stairwell of life is our lesson route filled with tough climbs and winding paths. We can't get stuck in the staircase; it's too dark and dreary. As the light bulb has been replaced, take advantage of the illumination and find your way out of darkness. The door to the next level awaits your arrival to higher heights in God's awesome plan for you.

Lydia met this juncture in her day-to-day living as see bumped into the Apostle Paul on the banks of the river. It was along the seashore that he often assembled for prayer. As Lydia was a seller of purple, she belonged to the guild of dyers and by virtue of this; her work brought her to the water's shore. Don't despise the landings that appear to be routine in your daily existence. They are often major factors in your ultimate breakthrough. As Paul ministered to the assembled women there, Lydia was in the number and the Lord opened her heart: and she received the gospel message. Just think your entire journey was to this point for all that you are to become.

She was a modest woman who further chose to lead her household to believe. What's truly remarkable about her is that her simplicity of heart made way for her to open her door to God's grace. Go ahead, open the door and embrace the new you – revived and refresh. Her spirit of hospitality comforted all those afflicted while spreading the Gospel message against the hostile region which prevailed during that period.

My prayer is that we will learn and grow so that we'll be prepared to increase others. In Lydia's conversion there are many points of interest. It was brought about by providential circumstances. For her, she was at the right place at the right time for hearing Paul - we find her at Philippi; providence, which is the handmaid of grace, led her to the right spot. Again, grace was preparing her soul for the blessing; grace preparing for grace. She did not know the Savior, but as a Jewess, she knew many truths which were excellent stair-steps to a full knowledge of Jesus. Note the words, **"Whose heart the Lord opened."** She did not open her own heart. Her prayers did not do it; Paul did not do it. The Lord Himself must open the heart, to receive the things which make for our peace. He alone can put the key into the hole of the door and open it, and get admittance for Himself. He is the heart's master as He is the heart's maker. Lord, evermore give us an open heart and open the eyes of our heart – so that we can see You. Open your heart to the Master's plan; **"Whose heart the Lord opened"** Acts 16:14.

Arise and shine for your light is come and the glory of the Lord is risen upon you. Receive His reintroduction to the grace of your feminine being. This word is for you…, Vanilla Now & Later is about your journey up the stairs of life. It has nothing to do with the candy I was offered in the staircase, as much as it shows the uphill climb to overcome adverse seasons that lock us all in the stairwell. How glorious it is to be standing at the top where God is showing His purpose for those seasons.

The stairwell is the fight for our future; one step at a time helps us make a giant leap for womankind. Do something for God...and do it big! Make your life good with fresh revelation of His divine purpose for you. Hopefully, the stairwell didn't scare the life out of you; it's just the vertical shaft around which the staircase was built – interestingly enough, it was truly meant to protect you.

Appendix

Suggested Readings and Resources

1. Keil and Delitzsch Commentary on the Old Testament: New Updated Edition, Copyright © 1996 by Hendrickson Publishers, Inc.
2. Spurgeon Daily Devotional
3. Wikipedia, the free encyclopedia
4. Clifford & Joyce Penner, The Gift Of Sex - A Christian Guide to Sexual Fulfillment. Waco, TX: Word Incorporated, 1981.
5. Munroe, Myles, In Pursuit of Purpose. Shippensburg, PA: Destiny Image Publishers, Inc., 1996.
6. Friedman, Manis. Doesn't Anyone Blush Anymore: Reclaiming Intimacy, Modesty and Sexuality. San Fransisco: HarperSan Fransisco, 1990.
7. Kaplan, Aryeh. Waters of Eden: The Mystery of the Mikvah. New York: NCSY/ Union of Orthodox Jewish Congregations of America, 1976.

About the Author

Tina Pamela Norton is an ordained minister of God's Holy Word. She was educated in the New York City school system and attended Taylor Business Institute, New York, NY where she received her Associate Degree in Accounting. She later attended The University of Maryland, Burlington County Community College, and Thomas Edison State College, Trenton, NJ.

The call on her life to full-time ministry shifted her academic pursuits. During this period, Rev. Norton attended Jericho Christian Training Center, Washington, DC, Mt. Leo Bible School, and Evangelical Christian Bible Institute, El Paso, TX. Rev. Norton trained in the United States Air Force Chaplaincy Program Lay Minister Certification. She holds her degree in Biblical Studies and is furthering her studies at Trinity College & Theological Seminary, Newburgh, Indiana.

For over sixteen years, Rev. Norton served as the Assistant Pastor of Word Alive Christian Center, Eastampton, NJ, Rev. Curtis G. Norton, Jr., Senior Pastor. Presently, she serves the Merrick Park Baptist Church as First Lady and Executive Pastor under girding the vision of her husband's assignment. Tina served the International Association of Free Women In Christ, Inc. as the Northeast Regional Vice-President.

She is the author of **Always A Lady** and has also co-authored two books with her husband entitled, **Foundations** and **Covenant Rules: A Marriage Manual**. In addition to this, Lady Tina is the founder of the Little Ladies Network, which is an organization designed to empower young girls, and teens for success in life. She also develops curriculum targeted for this special generation.

Tina Pamela Norton is the twenty five year life partner of Reverend Curtis George Norton. Together they raised two children, Pleasure and Kiya. She strategically fulfills her desire to impact lives by making herself an available instrument. Her life philosophy, **"BE REAL,"** is daily exhibited in her character, as she puts it, *"I'm working on being the best ME, I could ever be!"*

Website:www.nortonministries.com

Acknowledgements

Special thanks to Linda Fennell, Alyse Howard, Martin Christie, Tarence Farrell, and Attorney James Walker, Spirit & Life Music Group. My heart is full as I reflect upon the suggestion by Martin on the eve of the books' printing that was delayed as I was encouraged to write a song for the book. I'd also like to thank Pastor Leslie Christie who urged her husband's discussion and thus we have "Here I Am".

Once the lyrics were written, I gave them to Pastor Norton and he put the melody to it along with Alyse as he collaborated with Martin and I must say that I am overwhelmed with the process and the results. It is truly a song of peace. Thank you all so very much.

I must also thank my friends and family for their intercessory prayers: Pastors Casey and Wendy Treat, Pastor Esther Lundy, Pastor Gail Watson, Lady (Evangelist) Ledie Farmer, Elder Althea Williams, Rosanda Richardson, Elder Arlena Brazell, Min. Denise Lawrence, Min. Shelia Holmes, Min. Charlotte Ferguson,

Acknowledgements

Dahime Gordon, Elder Tina Baker, Pastor Phyllis Carter, Pastor Michael and Elder Tasha Baston, Pastor Beverley Roberts and Min. Shelia Robinson you all were my lifeline over this project, thanks again. Special thanks to Candace Sandy, Walter Zacharius and Kensington Publishing for expanding our vision; your input is invaluable as the future looks very, very bright.